EMPTINESS
AND THE LIFE - GIVING SWORD

IAIDO

MUSO JIKIDEN EISHIN-RYU

Technique, terminology, the sword, and insight.

EMPTINESS
AND THE LIFE-GIVING SWORD
Bahman Ebrahimi

EMPTINESS AND THE LIFE - GIVING SWORD

First printing : August 2013
Second edition: April 2014
Printed in: (Lynnwood) WA, USA

Registration number: 1112347 1112346
ISBN 978-1-4992-7134-8

TABLE OF CONTENT

"I humbly present my thoughts to you on the following matters and pray that you do not think of me as one who would consider himself as wise as you.

Your esteemed servant,
Hidetomo Nakadai"
From The Shogun's Scroll, by Stephen F Kaufman

It is my intent to present this information with the same humility as Hideto-mo Nakadai and hope that you will gain insight and success in your journey along the way.

Bahman Ebrahimi

i

IAIDO

Saya No Uchi No Kachi
The sword in the scabbard, winning without drawing

IAIDO (ee-eye-do) is an authentic sword art of reacting to a surprise attack by counter attacking with a katana, (Japanese sword), when peaceful negotiation fails.

Hayashizaki Jinsuke Minamoto Shigenobu (1542 or 1546-1621) is the founder of Iaido, not only for classifying a system of batto jutsu (sword-drawing techniques), but also for promoting the idea that practicing sword forms with a meditative focus can make one a better person, and benefit society as well.

The Tokugawa military Shogunate (1603-1867) united the country after a long period of civil conflict. Soon after, the samurai adapted from being warriors to being civilians in an effort to better serve the government. The Meiji government (post-feudal period from 1863-1912) abolished the shogunal class system (feudal class system) and forbid the wearing of swords after 1868. Although the samurai class continued to practice sword techniques, self-discipline and character building became even more important than the fighting skills.

Under the Meiji Restoration (1868-1911), Iaido became increasingly popular. Traditionally, only samurai men practiced long sword, but nowadays, both men and women, from around the world study Iaido.

The philosophy of Iaido is not to overcome the enemy, but to overcome one's self. Iaido technique is highly refined emphasizing simplicity, directness, and determination. Every unnecessary movement has been eliminated. As a result, authentic Iaido does not present well for demonstrations as it does not contain flashy or showy movements. This graceful and dignified art exemplifies Japanese Budo in strengthening and developing character.

Iaido is an authentic Budo that proved its martial values in times of battle and warfare. Its purpose is to develop awareness, centeredness, sincerity, calmness, and mental and physical harmony through the practice of traditional sword techniques.

IAIDO REIHO (method of bowing in Iaido)

REI (Bow)

Iaido begins and ends with REI (the bow)

Rei is a way of showing respect and humility. OTAGAI NI REI (students bow to each other at the end of the class), shows that both Iaido students are in harmony without difference or contradiction. REI in the Iaido dojo will indicate the beginning and ending of training. Swords are only presented during class time, which begins and ends with REI. Performing the REI keeps the dojo peaceful and calm.

During the bowing ceremony, the katana's tsuka (sword handle) should be kept out of right hand reach. Consequently, the katana is grasped with the right hand and the action considered non-aggressive.This rule applies when we display the sword on katana kake (sword stand). The tsuka points to the left.

In RITSU REI / TACHI REI (standing bow toward shinzen or shomen), Iaido ka holds the saya in the right hand. The katana should remain in its steady position while bowing. The right hand is almost 10cm away from the tsuba.

In ZA REI (kneeling bow) the katana is moved from the left hand to the right hand and rests at the right side of the body with the tsuka pointing forward. This makes the drawing almost impossible.

During the TO REI (bowing to the sword) in seiza (seated position) the katana is placed in front on the floor with the tsuka to the left. Omote (face of the sword) is down.This means that the Ha (cutting edge) faces the Iaido ka.

In standing to-rei, both hands holding the sword are in front of the body at face level. The tsuka on the left side ha (edge) faces the body. The katana should remain steady in front of the body while bowing.

The duration of the rei should be kept one or two seconds longer than the sensei. This shows a sense of integrity and respect to the sensei, kamiza (higher seat) and to oneself. When bowing, one should be in a state of mushin (no mind) and muga (no ego).

Katana Etiquette

The Katana was more than a weapon to the samurai. The Katana represented the samurai's soul and his duty to society. The samurai considered the sword a part of themselves which gave them freedom from fear. The sword represented moral values like patience, discipline, honor, loyalty, determination, simplicity, calmness, tolerance, wisdom, courage, respect and trust. As a result, a strict code of ethics and formality was created on how to wear, train, carry and display the katana. Integrity to oneself and respect to the sword was highly recommended at all time. This even includes when we talk about the Japanese sword. The actual life-giving sword is not to be misused or misinterpreted, displayed or practiced in public.

An Iaido ka maintains these rules to preserve tradition and not to gratify the ego. According to rules of conduct, the Iaido ka is supposed to lock and cover the sword after each training session as follows:

1.The sageo is used to fasten the tsuka and the saya.

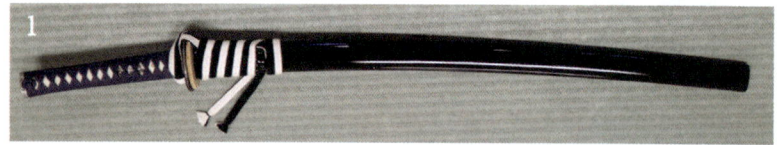

2.Place the sword inside a cloth bag and tie the opening of the bag.

3. Place the sword with cloth bag inside a Bukuro (Japanese formal katana cloth bag). The bag is fastened and tied with fusahimo (A fancy silk cord with tassels) in a traditional way.

4. The last step is to place the sword, wrapped in the Bukuro, in a heavy-duty double-sword padded bag.

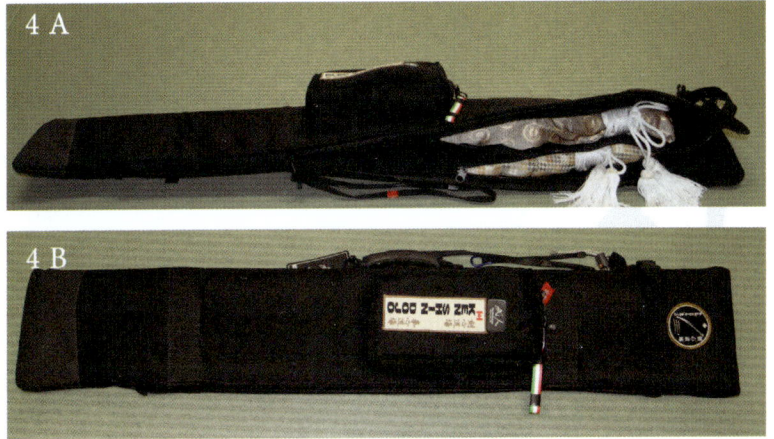

VISUAL GLOSSARY OF SWORD

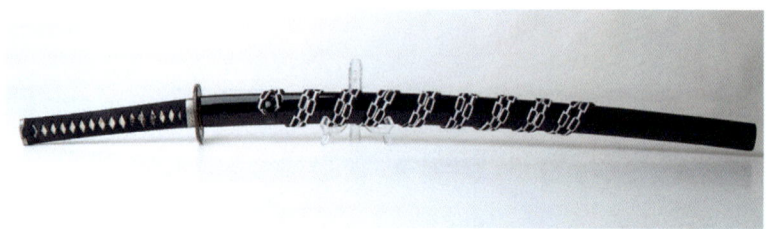

"The blade of the sword has only been displayed to provide information. In all other cases it is concealed in a show of respect to the art of Iaido."

Bahman Ebrahimi

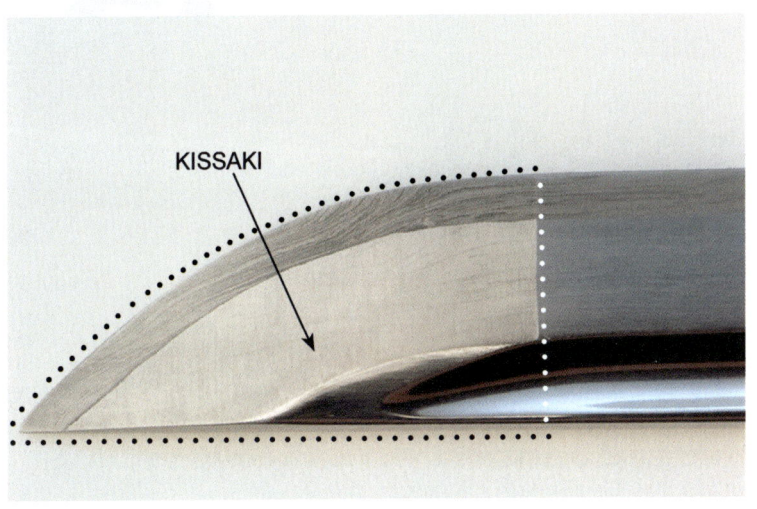

KISSAKI

The kissaki is the small point of a sword that has the ridge line (Shinogi)
There are different variations of length:

Ko kissaki: small point

Inokobi Kissaki: Medium Kissaki without Fukura

Chu kissaki: medium point

O kissaki: Large point

Kamasu kissaki: A large kissaki with an almost straight edge (no curve or fukura). Barracuda point.

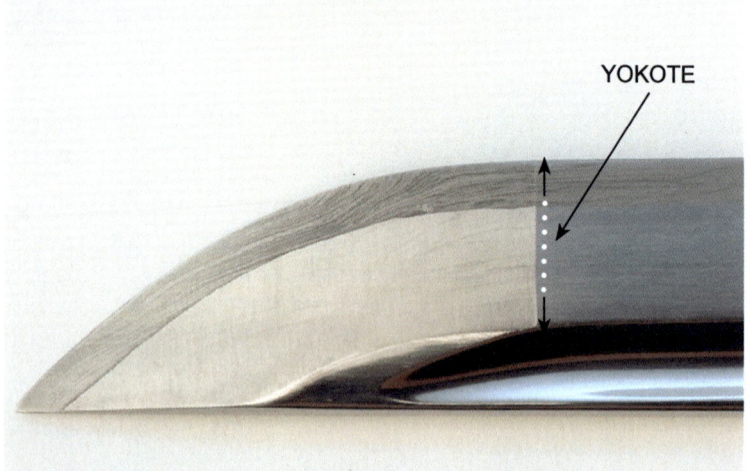

The Yokote is the line that divides the body of the blade (ji) with the tip (kissaki).

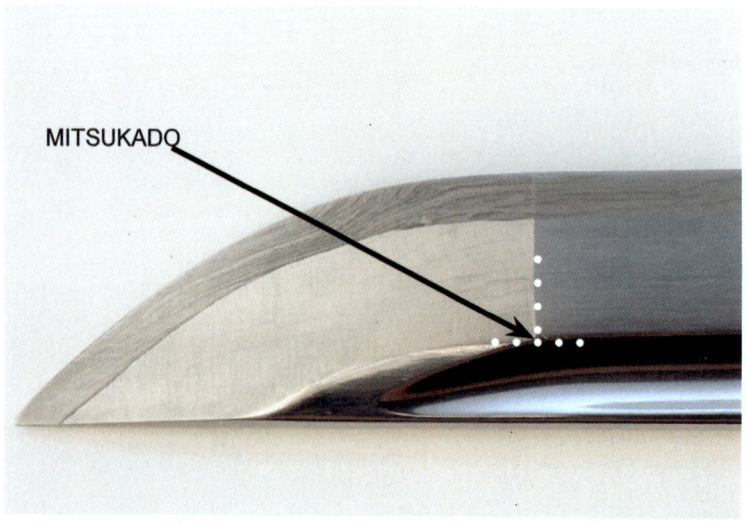

The Mitsukado is the point where the yokote, shinogi and the koshinogi are joined together.

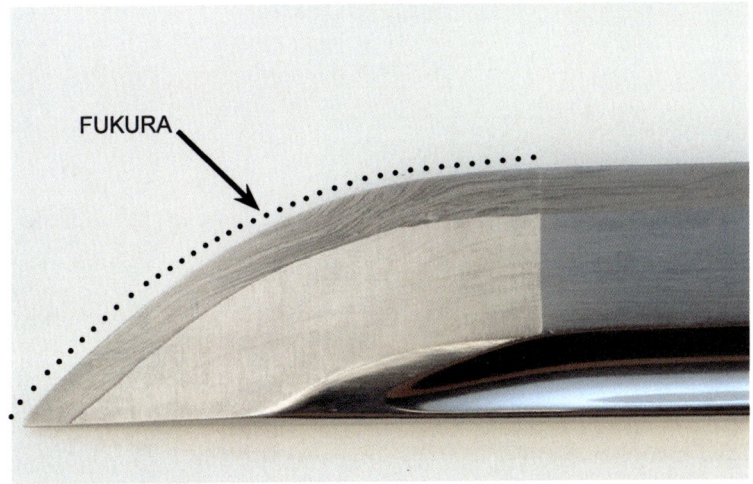

The Fukura refers to the roundness, the curvature of the cutting edge along the kissaki.

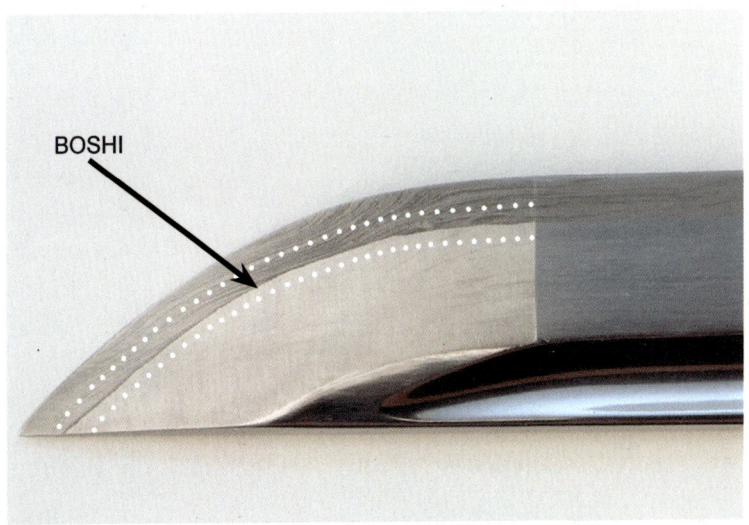

The Boshi is the hamon line along the kissaki of the blade.

TYPES OF BOSHI

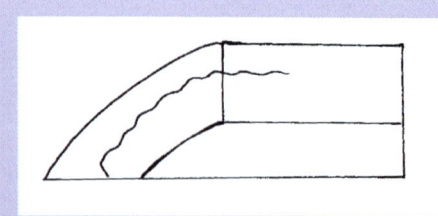

1. Midare-Komi
(Irregular wave)

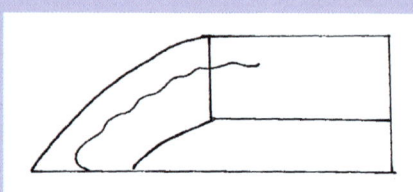

2. Komaru
(Small circle)

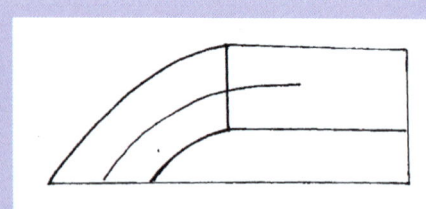

3. Yakizume
(does not turn-
back)

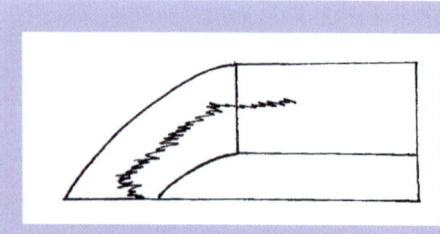

4. Hakikake
(Brushstroke)

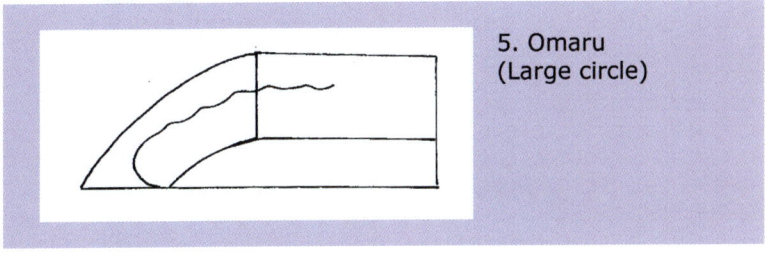

5. Omaru
(Large circle)

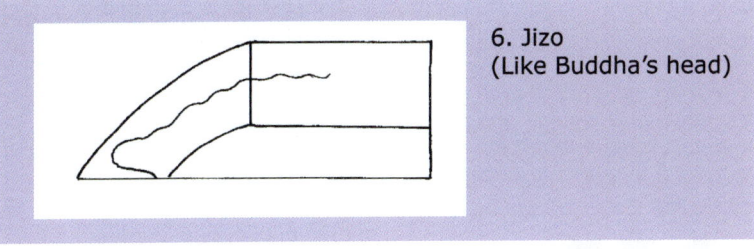

6. Jizo
(Like Buddha's head)

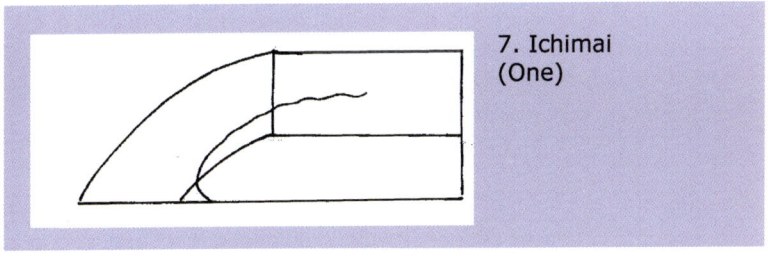

7. Ichimai
(One)

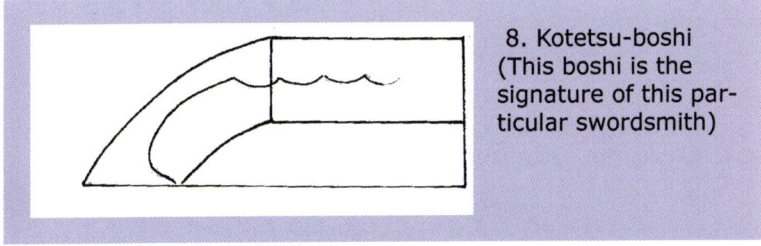

8. Kotetsu-boshi
(This boshi is the
signature of this par-
ticular swordsmith)

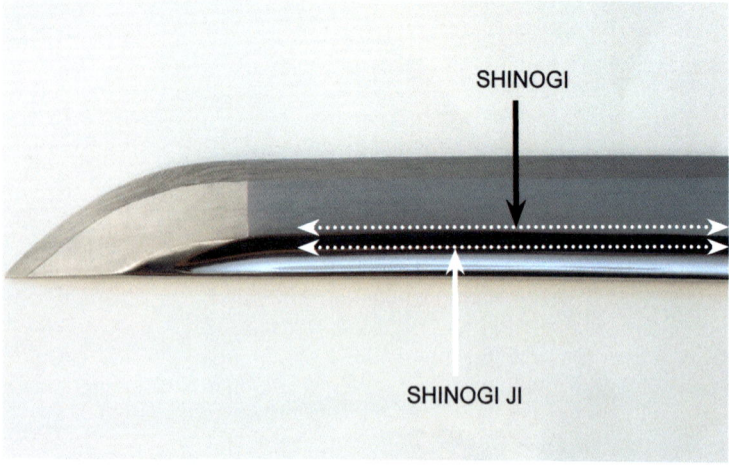

The Shinogi is a ridgeline located on the side of the blade between the mune and the ha. The Shinogi ji is the area between the mune and the shinogi. It is hard to locate shinogi ji in the picture above due to the big hi (Bo hi).

Tsukuri komi
The common shapes of the blade
 1-Hira-zukuri   Flat/ridgeless
2-Kiriha-zukuri   The ridgeline is closer to the cutting edge
3-Shinogi-zukuri The ridgeline is closer to the back
4-Kata kiriha   The kiriha is on one side and the other side is flat

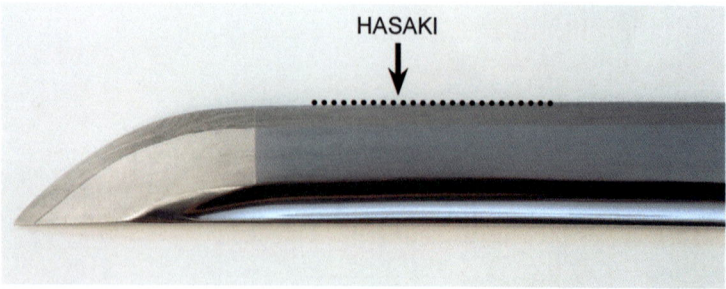

The Hasaki is the cutting edge of the sword.

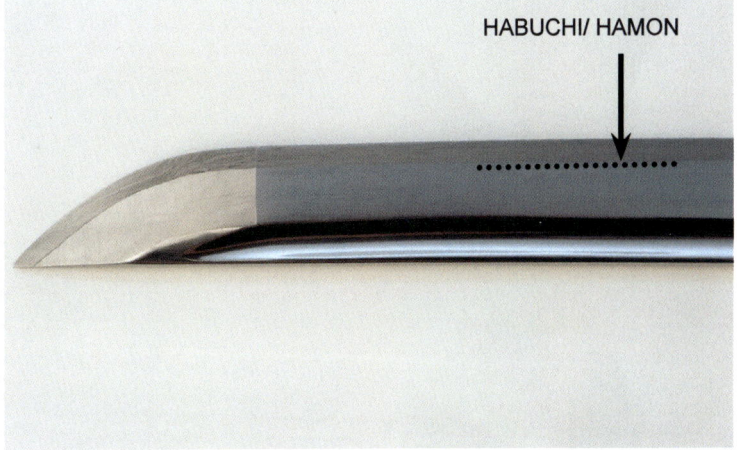

The Habuchi is the line of the hamon and the border between the hamon and ji.
The Hamon is the temper pattern along the habuchi as a result of the hardening process.

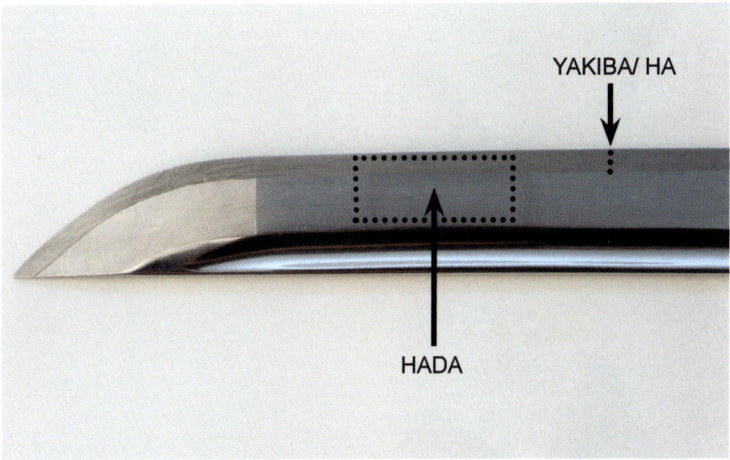

The Hada is the surface grain pattern produced by forging.
The Yakiba or Ha is the area near the cutting edge of the sword.

TYPES OF HADA

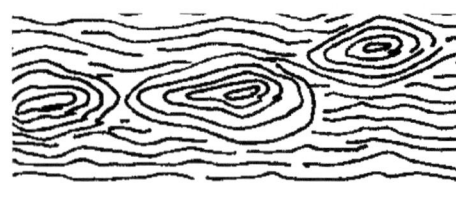

1. Itame
(Wood grain)

2. Mokume
(Itame with whorls)

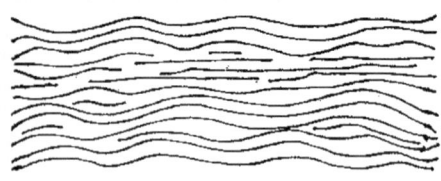

3. Ayasugi
(Regular wave lines)

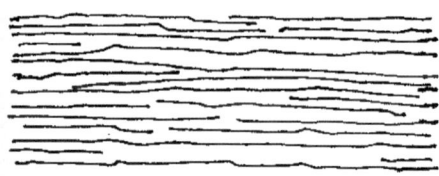

4. Masame
(Straight grain pat-
tern)

TYPES OF HAMON/HABUCHI

1. Suguha (Straight) ————————————
Suguha's width can be ~~classified as~~
classified as: Hiro-Suguha (Wide), Hoso-Suguha (Narrow), Chu-Sug-
uha (Medium)

2. Gunome (Series of waves)

3. Notare (Gentle waves)

4. Hakoba (Box-shaped)

5. Togari (Pointed)

6. Yahazu (Notched)

7. Sanbonsugi (Three Cedars)

8. Hitatsura (Full tempered)

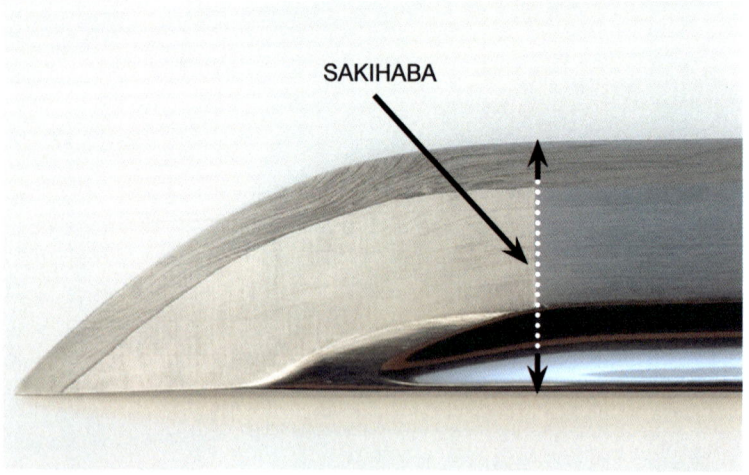

The Sakihaba is the width of the blade at the yokote.

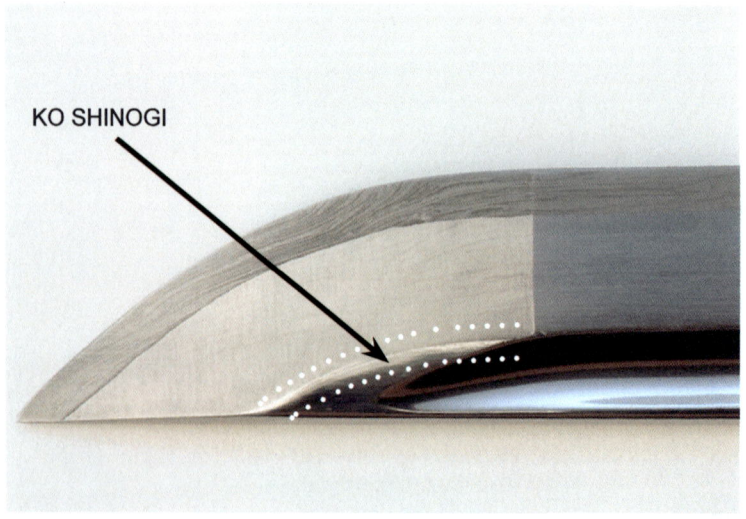

The Koshinogi is the extension of the shinogi at the kissaki.

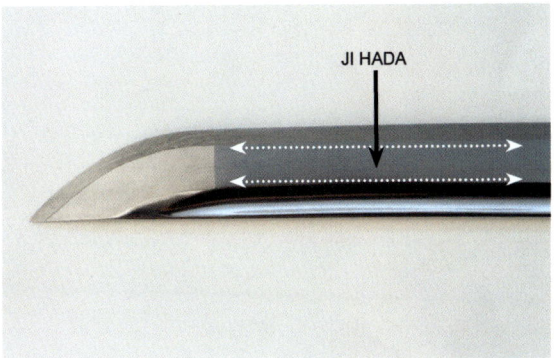

The Ji hada is the hada pattern produced in the forging in the ji area.

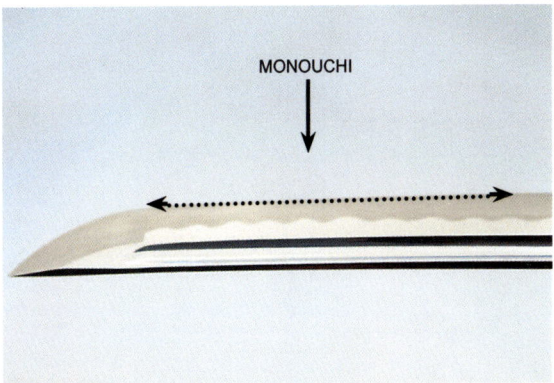

The Monouchi is the main cutting area of the blade.

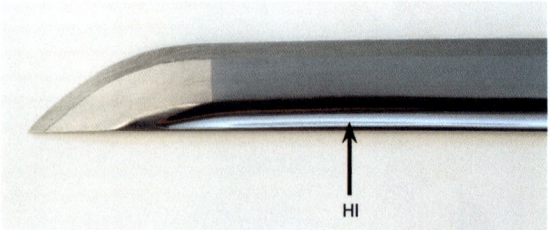

The Hi is the groove in the blade.

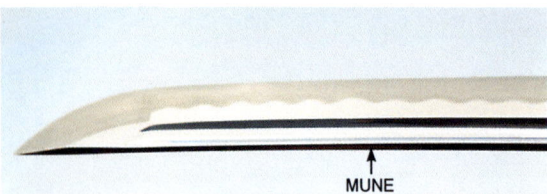

The Mune is the back ridge of the blade

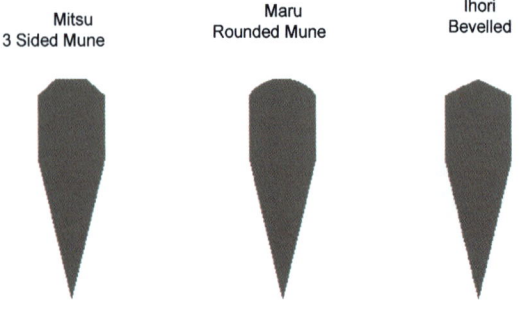

Mitsu
3 Sided Mune

Maru
Rounded Mune

Ihori
Bevelled

TYPES OF HI

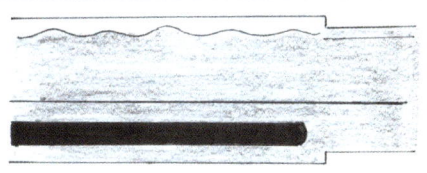

1-Bo-Hi
A wide, long groove down the length of the sword.

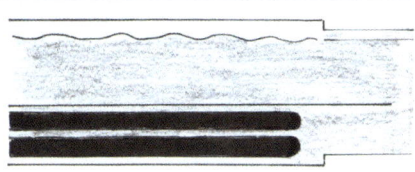

2-Futa-suji
Two long grooves along the blade

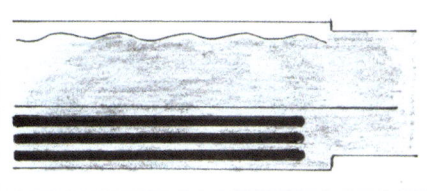

3-Missuji-Hi
Three long thin grooves

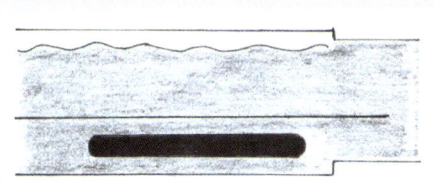

4-Maru-Dome
The groove has a squared end near the mune machi

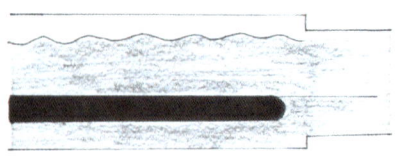

5-Kata-Chiri
Similar to the Bo-Hi
except the groove
touches the shinogi
line

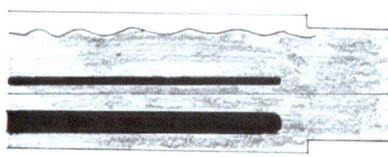

6-Soe-Hi
Bo-Hi and another
small groove over the
shinogi

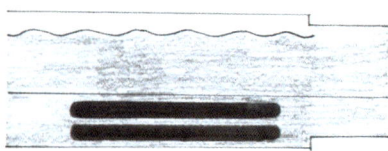

7-Gomabashi
Two short thin grooves
near the mune machi

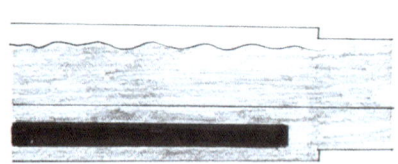

8-Kaku-Dome
The groove has a
squared end

9- Kaki Nagashi
The groove that runs part way along the tang

10- Kaki-Doshi
The groove that runs along the full length of the tang

TSUKA (Sword handle)

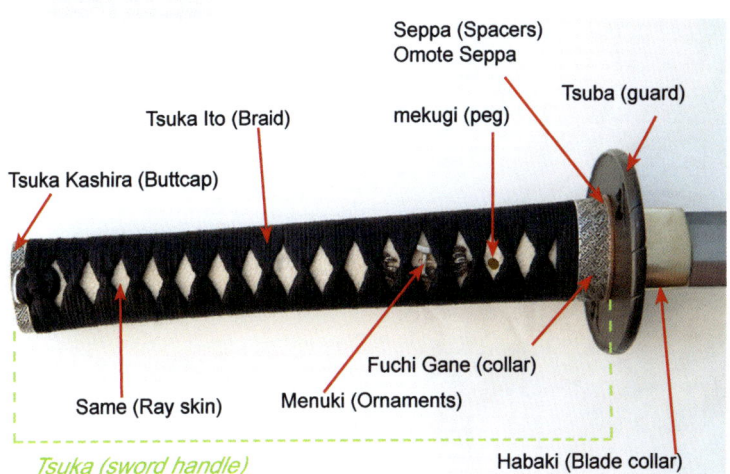

Seppa (Spacers)
Omote Seppa

Tsuba (guard)

Tsuka Ito (Braid)

mekugi (peg)

Tsuka Kashira (Buttcap)

Fuchi Gane (collar)

Same (Ray skin)

Menuki (Ornaments)

Tsuka (sword handle)

Habaki (Blade collar)

MEKUGI

Mekugi holds the tsuka and nakago together. It should be examined prior to practice and replaced if it is thin, broken, or appears weak. Ideally, the mekugi should be made of bamboo. Bamboo is flexible. Even if it breaks, the fiber core is resilient enough to prevent the blade from flinging across the room.

TSUKA BASIC SHAPES

1-Haichi Tsuka   Most common (as shown above)
2-Ryukko Tsuka   Almost hour glass shape
3-Imogata   Potato shape
4-Morozori   Almost following the angle of saya, common shape in tachi and handachi

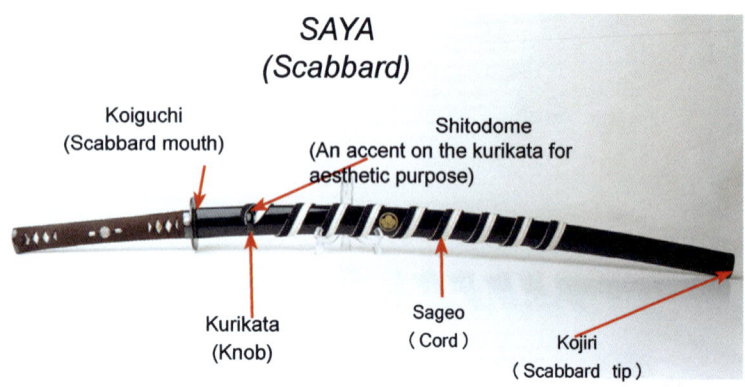

SAYA
(Scabbard)

Koiguchi
(Scabbard mouth)

Shitodome
(An accent on the kurikata for
aesthetic purpose)

Kurikata
(Knob)

Sageo
(Cord)

Kojiri
(Scabbard tip)

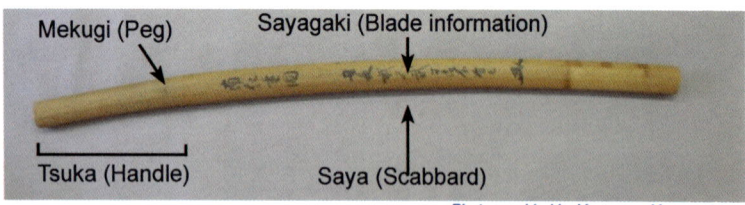

Mekugi (Peg)

Sayagaki (Blade information)

Tsuka (Handle)

Saya (Scabbard)

Photo provided by Yasumasa Yamamoto
(Tozando)

A Shirasaya is an undecorated plain wooden mounting. It is used to protect the sword blade when not in use and when not mounted. It may have saya-gaki (the information about the sword).

TSUBA
(Sword guard)
Omote side of the tsuba

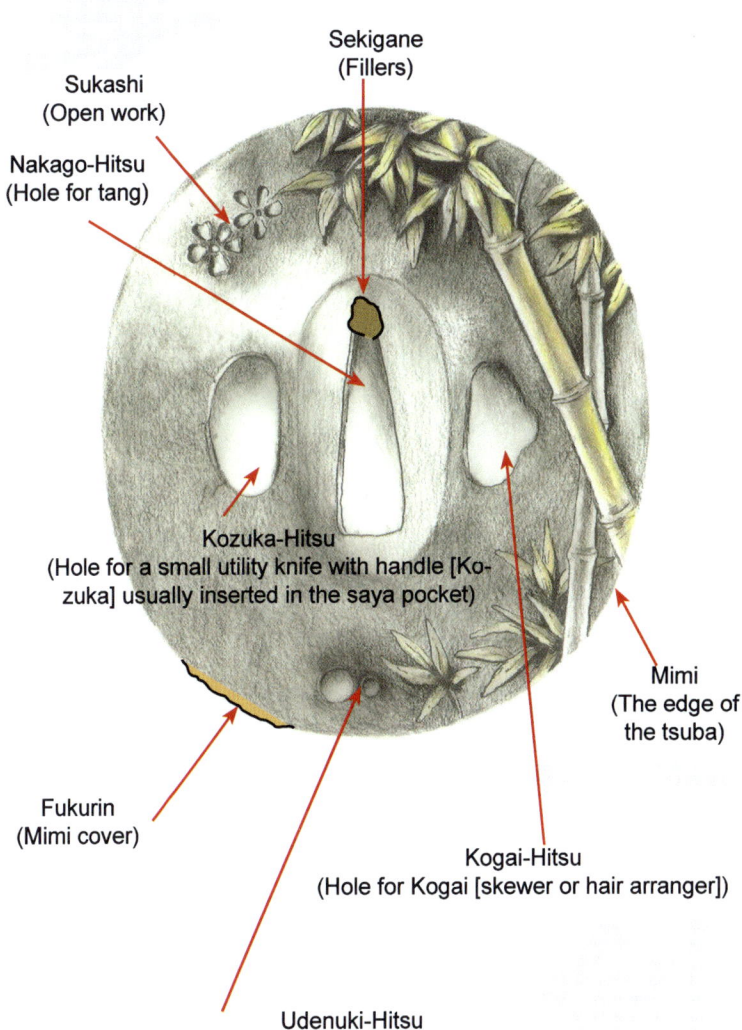

Sekigane
(Fillers)

Sukashi
(Open work)

Nakago-Hitsu
(Hole for tang)

Kozuka-Hitsu
(Hole for a small utility knife with handle [Ko-
zuka] usually inserted in the saya pocket)

Mimi
(The edge of
the tsuba)

Fukurin
(Mimi cover)

Kogai-Hitsu
(Hole for Kogai [skewer or hair arranger])

Udenuki-Hitsu
(One or two holes for tying the katana to the wrist while cutting)

Modified Tsuba painted by Akbar Goltapeh

TOSHIN NO SUNPO
BLADE AND NAKAGO MEASUREMENT

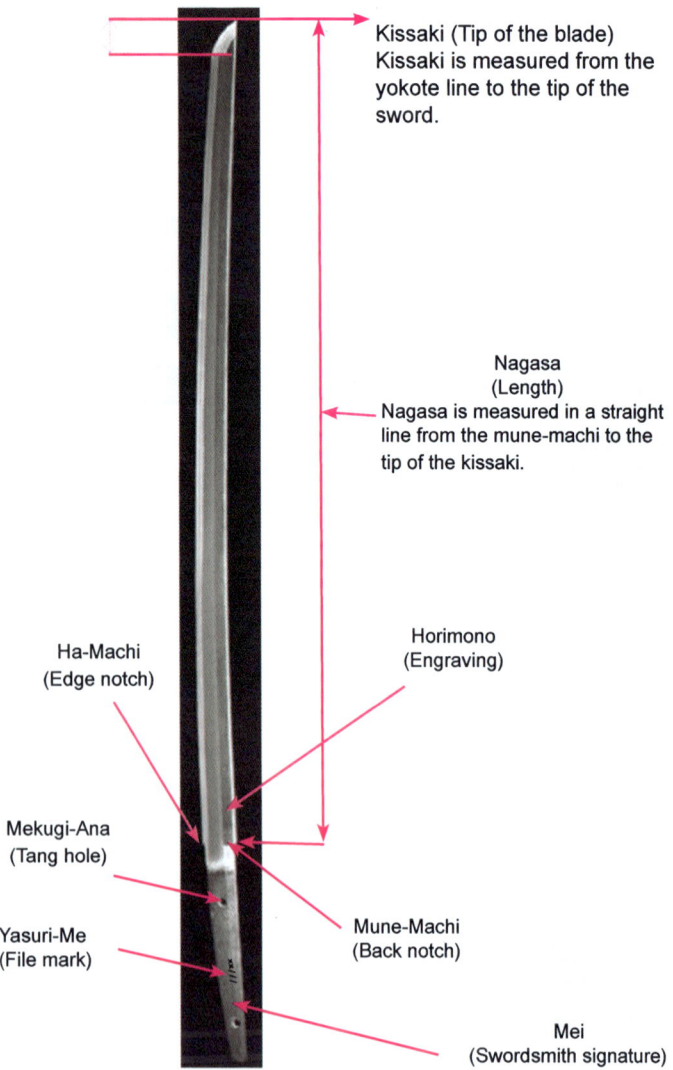

Kissaki (Tip of the blade)
Kissaki is measured from the
yokote line to the tip of the
sword.

Nagasa
(Length)
Nagasa is measured in a straight
line from the mune-machi to the
tip of the kissaki.

Horimono
(Engraving)

Ha-Machi
(Edge notch)

Mekugi-Ana
(Tang hole)

Yasuri-Me
(File mark)

Mune-Machi
(Back notch)

Mei
(Swordsmith signature)

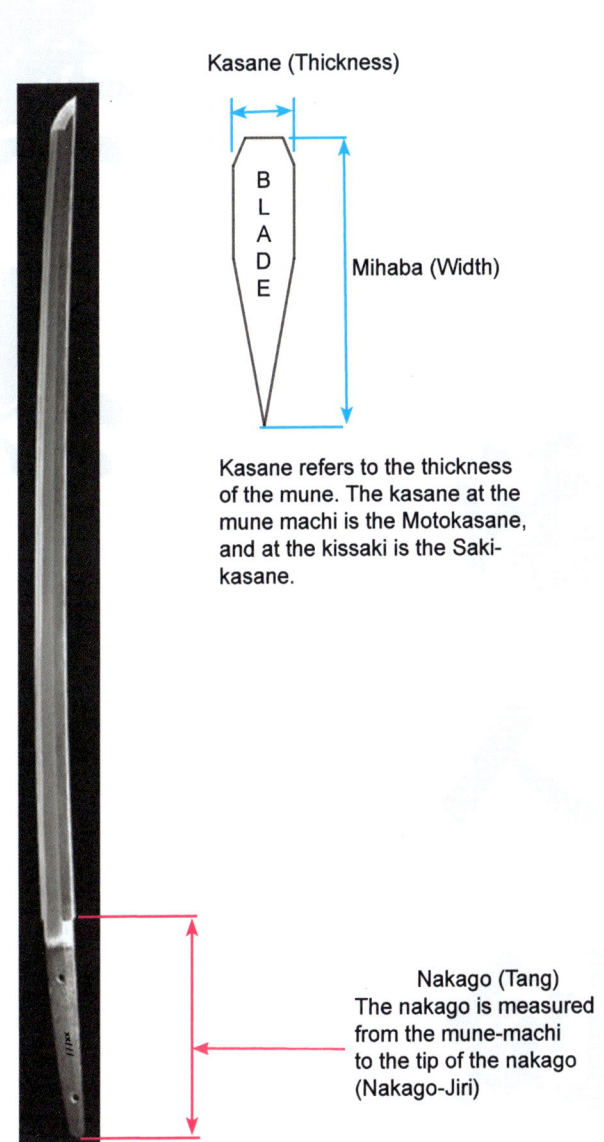

Kasane (Thickness)

BLADE

Mihaba (Width)

Kasane refers to the thickness of the mune. The kasane at the mune machi is the Motokasane, and at the kissaki is the Saki-kasane.

Nakago (Tang)
The nakago is measured from the mune-machi to the tip of the nakago (Nakago-Jiri)

Sori (Curvature)
Sori is measured from Mune (back of the
blade) at the widest point on a straight
line from the Mune-Machi to the tip of
the Kissaki.

TYPES OF SORI
1-Torri-Zori
The deepest part of the curvature is in
the center
2-Koshi-Zori
The deepest part of the curvature is
between the center of the blade and the
mune machi
3-Saki-Zori
The deepest part of the curvature is
between the center and the tip of the
sword, most commonly seen on Nagi-
nata.
4-Mu-Zori
A sword with no curvature or little curvature

Kissaki

Monouchi
15 to 20 cm

Shaku
30.2 cm/ 11.9 inches

Sun
1/10 of a shaku

Chu O

Bu
1/10 of a sun= 0.3 cm

Koshi
20 to 30 cm

Tsuba Moto
Blade nearest tsuba

Nakago

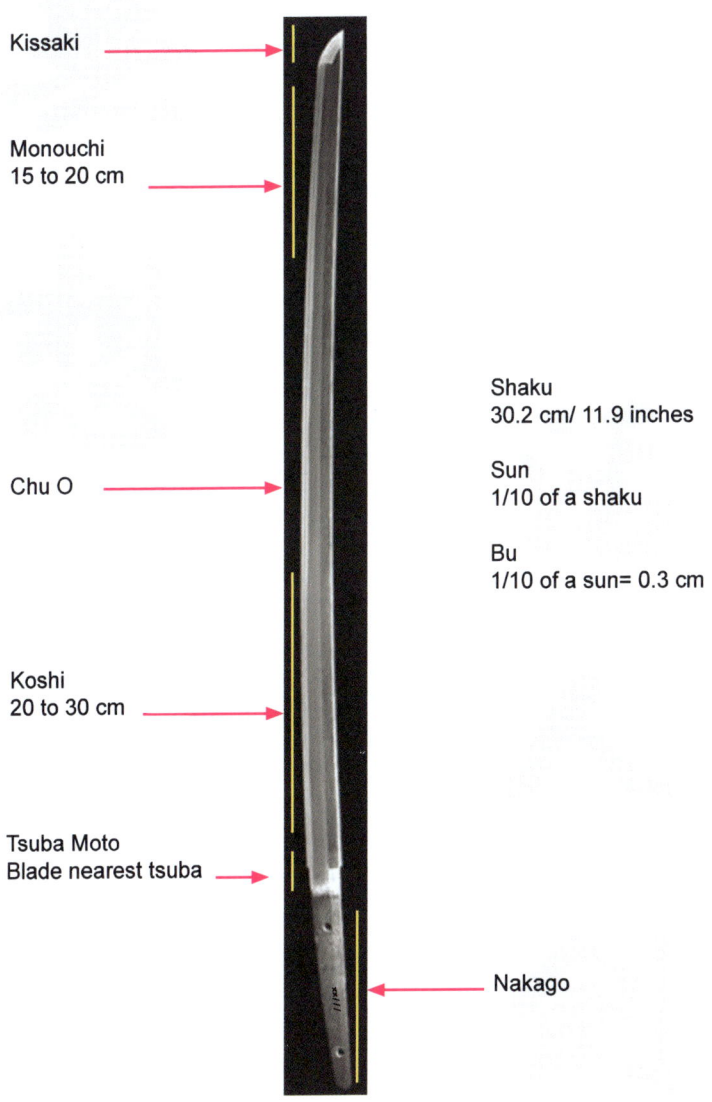

NAKAGO-JIRI
Common types of nakago

1. Kuri Jiri
(The end is rounded)

2. Kiri
(The end is square)

3. Ha Agari
(Similar to kuri jiri. The round end is deeper on the edge)

4. Iriyama Gata
(The end is angled)

YASURI-ME
Types of file marking
Note: Files can completely cover the tangs

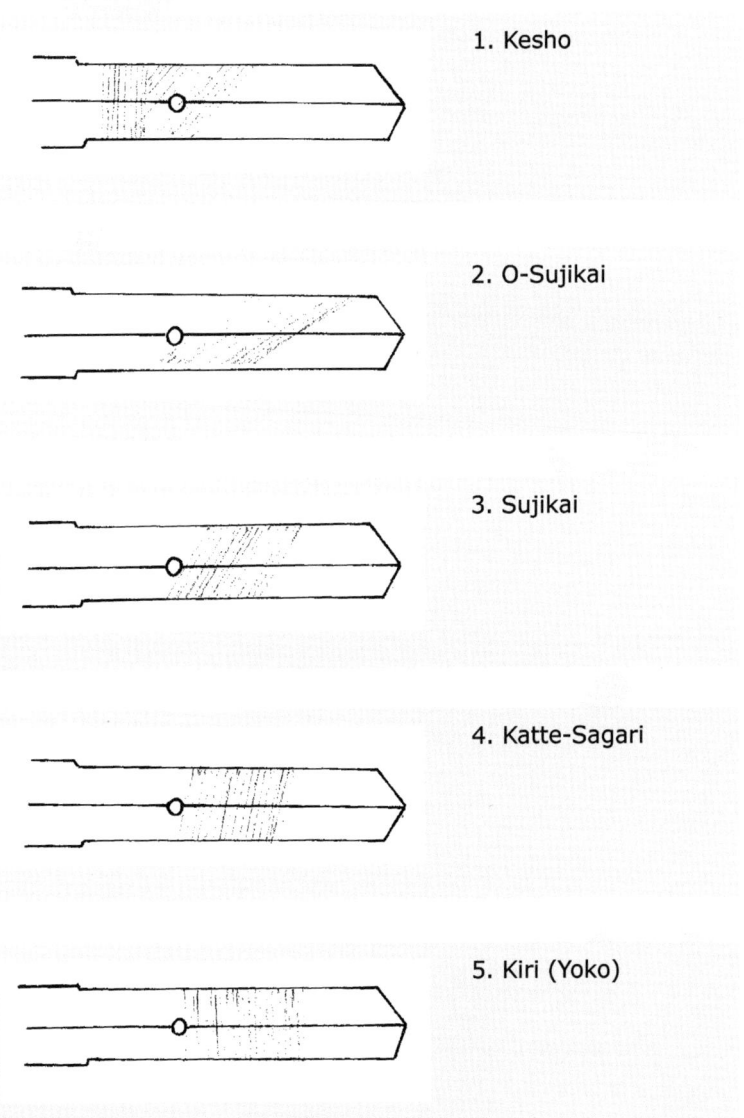

1. Kesho

2. O-Sujikai

3. Sujikai

4. Katte-Sagari

5. Kiri (Yoko)

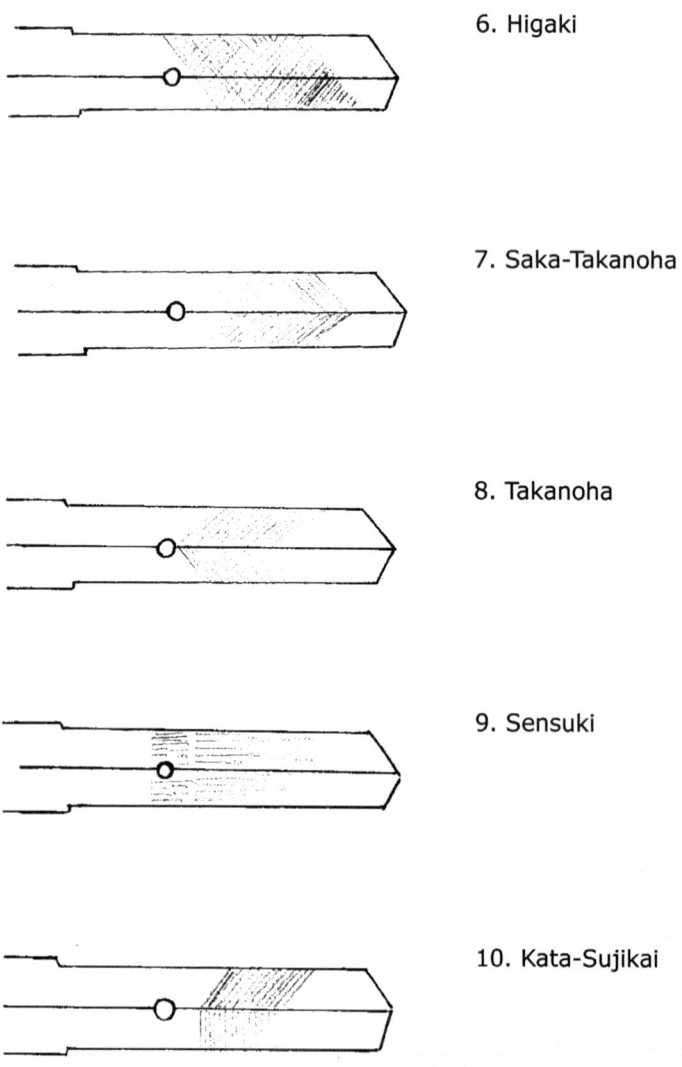

6. Higaki

7. Saka-Takanoha

8. Takanoha

9. Sensuki

10. Kata-Sujikai

無想

活人劍

GLOSSARY OF TERMS

Iaido – The traditional Japanese art of drawing and cutting with the Samurai sword.
I – Coexistence, sitting down facing each other, and a form of peaceful negotiation
Ai – Harmonious/adaptable
Do – Path or way to positively affect one's life
Muso Jikiden Eishin-Ryu – Peerless, direct transmission, true path style of Eishin
Hayashizaki Jinsuke Minamoto no Shigenobu
(1546 – 1621 AD)
Founder of Iaido. He promoted the idea of peaceful meditative intent.

PHILOSOPHICAL TERMS

In-yo – Yin and yang
Kobudo – Ancient martial ways
Kime – Focus
Kenwa kokoro nari – True heart, true sword
Katsu jin ken – Life-giving sword
Satsu jin ken – Life-taking sword
Budo – Way of martial arts
Bushido – Way of samurai
Muga – No ego
Munen – No thought (absent of conscious thought)
Mushin, Muso – No mind, no rationalization
Ki – Spirit, inner strength
Ki ken tai ichi – Spirit, sword, body, one
Saya no uchi no kachi/Saya no uchi de katsu – Scabbard, inside, victory (The sword in the saya) (winning without drawing)
Shu ha ri – Keep, Break, Leave. Memorize technique, question and understand, forget technique
Jo ha kyu – Slow, faster, fastest
Kiai – Shout
Kokyu – Breath, Breath power
Fudushin – Immovable mind, calm spirit
Suki – Weakness of the mind caused by astonishment, fear, doubt or hesitation. Also, a weakness in one's action or posture, which results from losing control of the center. Suki provides an opening for attack.

Giri – Duty or obligation of one person toward another
Fushin – Frozen mind
Mudana chikara – No unnecessary power or force
Mudana ugoki – No unnecessary movement/technique
Tsune ni ite, kyu ni awasu – Whatever we may be doing or wherever we may be, we must always be prepared for any eventuality
Dai kyo soku ke – Big, strong, fast and smooth
Sei to do – An action, no action. Calmness in movement

IAIDO TERMS

Iaido ka – A student of Iaido
Shinken shobu – Drawing and cutting with shinken in battle
Seiza – Kneeling/sitting
Tachi – To stand/standing
Metsuke – Point of observation, to look
Te no uchi – Grip on sword with fingers pulling into palm
Enzan no metsuke – Gaze at the far mountains
Saya okori – Movement of the scabbard during Furikaburi
Tsuba zeri ai – Sword tangle
Saya atari – Collision between the saya of two swordsmen
Saya biki – Moving the saya back with the left hand during the first cut
Saya banare – The moment kissaki comes out of the scabbard
Chiburi – Shaking off blood
O Chiburi – Large or circular chiburi
Yoko chiburi – Horizontal chiburi, move to the side
Chinugui – Wiping off the blood as is performed in ukenagashi or tsuke-komi
Batto – To unsheathe
Noto – Replacing the blade in the saya
Hayaosame – Faster version of regular noto; performed during advanced (oku) waza
Shimeru – Wringing, twisting the hand inward over the handle at the end of the cut
Tai Sabaki – Body movement
Ashi Sabaki – Foot or leg movement
Kiai/Kake Goe – Shout, yell

Ma ai – Distance, space, interval (in time)
A.   Chikama – Short distance
B.   Issoku itto no maai (Itto ma/Chuma) – Middle distance. One-foot, one-sword distance. Ito-ma is the distance equalling one step in order to make an effective cut.
C.   Toi ma ai – Long distance. The Iaido ka won't be able to reach each other.

Zanshin – Awareness, watchfulness, lingering heart
Junbitaiso – Warming up
Teki – Enemy
Aite – Opponent/partner
Kasso teki – Invisible enemy
Waza – Technique
Kata – Structured two person practice; form or pattern
Shitachi – The one who completes the sword, finishes the higher rank or teacher, and wins
Uchitachi – Entering sword attacker, loser, teacher higher rank
Bushi – Knight or samurai
Kuchi bushi – Mouthy warrior (talks too much)
Ni ho haba – A stance that is two steps in length
Keiko – Practice
Embu – Demonstration
Taikai – Big event
Tameshigiri – Test cutting
Tasuki Sabaki – Special way of tying the tasuki around the neck to put the Sode out of the way
Kizu – Wound, cut, or flaws on the sword
Hakama sabaki – Hakama arrangment before seiza
Hiki waza – Moving-back sword techniques
Junbitaiso – Warm-up cuts
Junbitaiso o hagime masu – Begin the warm-up
Junbitaiso o owarimasu – Warm-up finished

ETIQUETTE

Reiho – Etiquette, method of bowing
Reishiki – Same as above
Rei – Bow
Za rei – Kneeling bow
Tachi rei/Ritsu rei – Standing bow
Kamiza ni rei – Bow to kamiza

Joseki ni rei – Bow to the high section of the dojo
Otegai ni rei – Bow to each other
Shinzen ni rei – Bow to shinzen (said by sempai)
Sensei ni rei – Bow to teacher (s)
Mokuso – Close the eyes (said by sensei or higher sempai)
To Rei – Bow to sword
Naore – As you were
Hajime no saho – Beginning etiquette
Owari no saho – Finishing etiquette
Moku rei – Bow with slight nod

SWORD EQUIPMENT/ACCESSORIES

Katana yohin – Sword accessories
Katana kake – Sword stand
Katana makura – Pillow for sword
Katana bukuro – A Japanese formal katana cloth bag
Fusa himo – A fancy cord usually made of silk with tassels
Katana tei re – Cleaning kit and maintenance
Mekugi nuki – Copper hammer and pin
Uchiko – Ball of stone powder
Susudake – Aged and smoked bamboo for mekugi
Nugui gami – Wiping paper for sword
Abura – A rust preventive oil called choji or clove oil
Abura Nuguishi – Paper used to spread oil over the blade
Fukurin – Tsuba's rim cover

JAPANESE TERMS

Domo arigato gozaimasu – Thank you very much (present tense)
Domo arigato gozaimashita – Thank you very much, said at the end of the class to each other, (past tense)
Dozo – Please go ahead
Sumimasen – Excuse me (to attract attention i.e. while trying to get through a crowd of people)
Hajime – Start
Yame/Owari – Stop
Hai – Yes
Do itashimashite – Don't mention it
Moichido – Once more
Yoshi – Good

Yoroshi – Good, very nice
Onegai Shimas – Please work with me
Oshiete kudasai – Please teach me
Owari masu – Finish, end
Ato – Move back/behind/later
Hayaku – Quickly
Mate – Wait
Mawatte – Turn around
Yukuri – Slow
Motto Yukuri – More slowly
O Tsukare Sama Deshita – An expression of thanks. You have become tired because of all the teaching you have done.
Wakarimasu ka? – Do you understand?
Wakarimasu – I understand (present tense)
Wakarimashita – I understood
Wakarimasen – I don't understand
Ohayo gozaimasu – Good morning
Konnichiwa – Good day
Konbanwa – Good evening
Oyasumi nasai – Good night
Kensei – Sword saint (This refers to their skills with the sword, not their character. They can have positive or negative personality).
Katana wo motte – Get your sword
Toko/Katana Kaji – Swordsmith

CLOTHING

Iai gi – Practice clothing for upper body (not referred to as just "gi" in Japan, which means "to wear")

Monstuki – Clothing for upper body that has long sleeves and a mon (family crest) on it.

Juban – Undergarment worn below monstuki

Uwa gi – Practice top

Keiko gi – The top of the training uniform.

Kamishimo – Over-vest/Jacket with exaggerated shoulders

Haori – Over jacket

Hakama – A traditional type of pleated pants

Himo – Straps/cords of Hakama

Hera – Peg in the back of Hakama

Matadachi – Split on side of Hakama

Zori – Sandals

Tabi – Japanese socks

Tenugui – Small hand cloth to wipe face

Furoshiki – Japanese cloth for keeping uniform clean during the folding

Zekken – Chest patch

Kesa – Lapel

Sode – Sleeves

Obi – Belt

MEANING OF HAKAMA'S PLEATS

(Other interpretations may exist)
Front of the hakama
Jin – Benevolence/ Mercy
Gi – Justice/ Righteousness
Rei – Etiquette/ Manners
Chi – Intelligence/ Wisdom
Shin – Faithfulness/ Trustfulness
Bak of the hakama
Chu – Loyalty
Kou – Piety

THE BODY

Tai – Body
Ashikubi – Ankle
Ashi Yubi – Toes
Te – Hand
Tekubi – Wrist
Ude – Arm
Hiji – Elbow
Kata – Shoulder
Atama – Head
Me – Eye
Kubi – Neck
Nodo – Throat
Sui Getsu – Solar plexus
Mune – Chest
Ura – Back of hand
Yubi – Finger/toe

Koshi – Hip
Hara – Abdomen
Ashi – Foot
Tanden – Lower abdomen
Hiza – Knee
Kuchi – Mouth
Komekami – Temples
Teisoku – Sole of the foot
Chusoku – Ball of the foot
Kakato – Heel of the foot
Nakazumi – Centerline of the body
Karada no chusin – Center of the body

DIRECTIONS

Mae – Forward
Migi – Right
Hidari – Left
Ushiro – Behind, to the rear
Gedan – Low
Chudan – Middle
Jodan – High
Ichi Mon ji – A straight line
Tate ichi mon ji – A vertical line
Yoko ichi mon ji – A horizontal line
Omote – Front
Yoko itto – Same as above
Heiko – Parallel
Kakudo – Angle
Naname – Diagonal
Ura – Back
Shomen – Straight a head
Uchi – Inside
Soto – Outside
Yoko – Horizontal, to the side
Gyaku – Reverse, opposite
Do – Degrees
Suichokku – Perpendicular
Chokkaku – 90 degree angle
Yon ju go do – 45 degree angle

ASHI SABAKI (FOOTWORK)

Footwork is the most important part of Japanese swordsmanship. It gives good balance and helps keep the core or trunk centered.

Tachi – Standing
Seiza – Kneeling on both shins
Iai Hiza – Kneeling on one shin
Sei tai/Omotemi – Forward stance
Han mi – Half-forward stance
Iri mi – Back stance
Ayumi ashi – Walking foot. Placing one foot in front of the other.
Tsugi ashi – Connecting foot. Moving forward with one foot (either the left or the right) always in front and pulling the back foot forward.
Tora bashiri – Tiger running. Running in small steps, placing one foot in front of the other.
Suriashi – Sliding step. Stepping without lifting up the toes
Ato – Step back
Hiraki ashi – Step to the side
Shikko – Walking or moving on the knees from seiza.

RANKS AND TITLES

Soke – Headmaster of a style
Shihan – Head or senior master
Sensei – Instructor
Sempai – Senior student
Kohai – Junior student
Dan Degree (Black belt), from 1 to 10
shodan, nidan, sandan, yondan, godan, rokudan, nanadan, hachidan, kudan, judan
Yuudansha – Members with Dan grades
Mudansha/ Dangai – Members without Dan grades – (does not indicate an individual's level of skill)
Hanshi – Master teacher (8 Dan & above)
Kyoshi – High ranking teacher (7 to 8 Dan)
Renshi – Acclaimed instructor or teacher (6 to 7 Dan)
Kaicho – Head of the organization
Kancho – Owner of school (Class, building, hall)

KEN SABAKI (SWORD WORK)

Heiho – Old term for fencing and sword techniques
Kiri – Cut
Kesagiri – Diagonal downward cut
Katate kesagiri – One handed diagonal cut
Morote kesagiri – Two handed diagonal cut
Kirioroshi – Downward cutting motion, straight down
Nukitsuke – Drawing the sword from its scabbard (horizontal cut)
Furikaburi – Raising the sword above the head
Sune gakoi – Block to protect the leg (shin)
Tsuki – Thrust
Uchi – Strike
Yoko ichi monji – Horizontal cut   YOKO = SIDE   ICHI MONJI = ONE DIRECTION) STRAIGHT
Gyaku kessagiri – Inverted diagonal upward cut
Tome te – Stopping hand
Kiri te – Finishing hand
Shini te – Hand position that does not allow a cut. Dead hand
Seme te – Pushing hand. Pressing forward with the blade
Nobi te - Same as shini te
Soete giri – The way of cutting in tatehiza. (one hand on blade)
Tameshigiri – Test cutting (not done in Eishin Ryu Iaido)
Osame to – Replacing sword into saya
Uke nagashi – Receive and deflect
Koshi guruma – Cutting in a horizontal line just below the belly button.
Do giri – Cutting a horizontal line on the belly
O-Chiburi – Large, circular chiburi
Yoko-Chiburi – Side chiburi
Hiki giri – Pulling-back cut
Morote tsuki – Two-handed sword thrust
Katate tsuki – One-handed sword thrust
Tsuka ate – Strike with the sword handle
Saya ate – Strike with the saya
Hasuji – Blade angle and cutting angle
Haneage – Flipping up the blade after soete giri

KAMAE (COMBATIVE POSTURES)
SWORD POSITIONS AND POSTURES

Teito – Holding the sword loose by the left side. Also used when the sword is in the belt and both hands loose at side

Te to – Holding the sword loose by the left side lower than teito

Teito Shisei – Holding the sword by the left side as if in the obi with thumb on Tsuba

Keito – Same as teito shisei

Taito – Putting the sword into the belt

Datto – Taking the sword from the belt

Seigan/chudan no kamae – Kissaki is at throat height

Jodan no kamae – Sword is at a 45 degree angle above the head

Gedan no kamae – Lower level, kissaki is at the height of the kneecap

Waki no kamae – Sword pointed down and back usually on the right side of the body. Left hand is just below the belly button. The kissaki can't be seen from the front.

Hasso no kamae – Sword by the side of the head. (Sword on right side) left foot forward. Sword is at almost 40 to 60 degree.

Kuruma no kamae – Like waki gamae, blade horizontal

Kasumi no kamae – Mist position

Kongo – Blade vertical in front of the face

SWORD NAMES

Bokken/Bokuto – Wooden katana
Iaito – Practice sword for Iaido
Shinken – Live blade
Katana – Japanese sword with blade mounted edge up
Daito – Great sword (katana)
Daisho – Set of two swords
Tanto – Dagger
Wakizashi – Short sword
Gunto – War sword (WWII)
Shinto – New sword (1600-1870)
Kozuka – Small knife usually inserted in the scabbard pocket. Consists of a hitsu (handle) and a ho (blade)
Shoto – Smaller sword
Aikuchi – Smaller wakizashi with no tsuba same as Hamidashi
Kazu Uchimono – Mass-produced blades of little artistic quality
Shi komi zue – Cane sword
Suri age – Blade that has been shortened (The blade will be less valuable)
Shira saya – Undecorated wood storage mount including tsuka and saya
Shinobi Gatana/Ninja to – Straight blade sword used by Ninja

SIDE OF THE SWORD

Sashi Omote - The side that faces out from the hip. Usually this side is signed by the sword maker
Sashi Ura – Side that faces the hip
Omote seppa – Seppa near Fuchi
Ura seppa – Seppa near Habaki
Tsuba Omote - Side of the tsuba near the Fuchi
Tsuba Ura - Side of the tsuba near the Habaki

DOJO ARRANGEMENT

Shomen – Front of room
Shinzen, Kamiza – Altar
Joseki – Upper side
Shimozeki, Shimoza – Lower side

WAZA IN MUSO JIKIDEN EISHIN RYU IAIDO

STANDING FORMS

BATTO HO

1. Junto sono ichi
2. Junto sono ni
3. Tsuigekito
4. Shato
5. Shihoto sono ichi
6. Shihoto sono ni
7. Zantotsuto

OKU NO KATA

1. Zenteki gyakuto
2. Tatekito
3. Koteki gyakuto
4. Koteki nukiuchi

OKU IAI

1. Yukizure
2. Tsuredachi
3. So Makuri
4. So Dome
5. Shinobu
6. Yukichigai
7. Sodesuri Gaeshi
8. Moniri
9. Kabezoi
10. Ukenagashi
Itomagoi sono ichi
Itomagoi sono ni
Itomagoi sono san

BANGAI NO BU

1. Hayanami
2. Raiden
3. Jinrai
4. Akumabarai

SEATED FORMS

SEIZA NO BU

1. Mae
2. Migi
3. Hidari
4. Ushiro
5. Yaegaki
6. Ukenagashi
7. Kaishaku
8. Tsukekomi
9. Tsukikage
10. Oikaze
11. Nukiuchi

TATE HIZA NO BU

1. Yokogumo
2. Toraissoku
3. Inazuma
4. Ukigumo
5. Oroshi
6. Iwanami
7. Urokogaeshi
8. Namigaeshi
9. Takiotoshi
10. Makko

IWAZA NO BU

1. Kasumi
2. Sunegakoi
3. Tozume
4. Towaki
5. Shihogiri
6. Tanashita
7. Ryozume
8. Torabashiri

IAIDO TOHO

1. Maegiri (Eishin ryu)
2. Zengogiri (Mugai ryu)
3. Kiriage (Shindo Munen ryu)
4. Shihogiri (Suio ryu)
5. Kissakigaeshi (Hoki ryu)

WAZA IN MUSO JIKIDEN EISHIN RYU
BATTO HO(KIHON NO KATA)

Basic technique

Batto Ho is considered basic, fundamental and essential for Ashi, Tai and Ken Sabaki. The Iaido ka needs several years of Batto Ho study along with Seiza no bu to move to advanced level.

Drawing forms are as follows:

1-Ipponme	Junto sono ichi	Regular sword #1
2-Nihonme	Junto sono ni	Regular sword #2
3-Sanbonme	Tsuigekito	Pursuing sword
4-Yonhonme	Shato	Angular sword
5-Gohonme	Shihoto sono ichi	Four directional cut #1
6-Ropponme	Shihoto sono ni	Four directional cut #2
7-Nanahonme	Zantotsuto	Cut and thrust

BATTO HO (OKU NO KATA)

Advance techniques.
Oku means deep inside(A deep insight)
Battle ready sword techniques.
Okuno kata is part of Batto Ho No Bu. It is considered a higher level transmission.

There are three important elements in Okuno Kata:
1. Shizentai. Starting from a walking motion. Hands are loose on both sides during the walking motion.
2. HAYAOSAME. A fast version of Osame to, which demands a high level of concentration and control. This particular re-sheathing is done silently with minimum or almost no contact of the sword edge with the sides of the saya.
3. KASHIRA. The right hand stays on the kashira while moving back to the starting point.

Oku No Kata are as follows:

1-Ipponme	Zenteki Gyakuto	Forward enemy inverse cut
2-Nihonme	Tatekito	Multiple opponents cut
3-Sanbonme	Koteki Gyakuto	Rear enemy inverse cut
4-Yonhonme	Koteki Nukiuchi	Rear enemy strike

SEIZA NO BU

Seated set is still considered basic level; however, it is recognized as the most important set in Iaido. Iaido ka is required to reflect and spend several years practicing the seiza no bu along with batto ho before moving to the next level.

Seiza forms are as follows:

1-Ipponme	Mae	Forward
2-Nihonme	Migi	Right
3-Sanbonme	Hidari	Left
4-Yonhonme	Ushiro	Rear
5-Gohonme	Yaegaki	Eightfold fence
6-Ropponme	Ukenagashi	Parrying
7-Nanahonme	Kaishaku	Assisting at seppuku
8-Hachihonme	Tsukekomi	Pursuit
9-Kyuhonme	Tsukikage	Moon shadow
10-Jupponme	Oikaze	Chasing wind
11-Juipponme	Nukiuchi	Draw and strike

TATEHIZA NO BU

Tatehiza is half-seated set, which includes extremely difficult movements. Tatehiza it categorized as highly advanced techniques. The waza includes half-kneeling and battle-ready sitting positions. These sets created enough mobility with good posture when a samurai wore armour, which was not flexible.

Tatehiza forms are as follows:

1-Ipponme	Yokogumo	Horizontal cloud
2-Nihonme	Toraisoku	Tiger's step
3-Sanbonme	Inazuma	Lightning
4-Yonhonme	Ukigumo	Floating clouds
5-Gohonme	Oroshi	Mountain wind
6-Ropponme	Iwanami	Rock and waves
7-Nanahonme	Urokogaeshi	Fish scale flip
8-Hachihonme	Namigaeshi	Flipping waves
9-Kyuhonme	Takiotosho	Flowing waterfall
10-Juponme	Makko	Facing front

OKU IAI NO BU
TACHIWAZA

These standing waza sets are intended for advanced Iaido ka and performed from walking. Tachiwaza (Standing waza) is included in the Eishin-Ryu at the higher level transmission. These waza are performed from a standing position with the same three elements that exist in Okuno Kata. Note: the last three techniques listed below are NOT performed from a standing position; they are from a seated position.

Oku iai/Tachi waza forms are as follows:

1-Ipponme	Yukizure	Accompaniment
2-Nihonme	Tsuredachi	Companions
3-Sanbonme	So Makuri	Complete flipping
4-Yonhonme	So Dome	Full stop
5-Gohonme	Shinobu	Invisible action
6-Ropponme	Yukichigai	Opposite direction
7-Nanahonme	Sodesuri Gaeshi	Sleeve turns
8-Hachihonme	Moniri	Entering the gate
9-Kyuhonme	Kabezoe	Between the walls
10-Juponme	Ukenagashi	Parrying
11-Juipponme	Itomagoi so no ichi	Farewell visit #1
12-Junihonme	Itomagoi so no ni	Farewell visit #2
13-Jusanbonme	Itomagoi so no san	Farewell visit #3

OKU IAI NO BU
IWAZA

These secret forms are characterized as Tatehiza forms with the Hayaosame (fast version Osame to). The techniques were created to function in areas with obstructions. Iwaza no bu includes highly advanced sets **Iwaza no bu forms are as follows:**

1. Ipponme	Kasumi	Mist
2. Nihonme	Sunegakoi	Shin block
3. Sanbonme	Tozume	Near the door
4. Yonhonme	Towaki	Beside the doorway
5. Gohonme	Shihogiri	Four directional cut
6. Ropponme	Tanashita	Beneath the ledge
7. Nanahonme	Ryozume	Blocked on both side
8. Hachihonme	Torabashiri	Tiger run

BANGAI NO BU

Extra set.

Bangai no bu was created to deal with multiple opponents. Bangai no bu has combinations of Eishin-Ryu standing forms except the fourth waza, which is completely new.

Bangai no bu forms are as follows:

1. Ipponme	Hayanami	Fast wave
2. Nihonme	Raiden	Thunder and lightning
3. Sanbonme	Jinrai	Thunderclap
4. Yonhonme	Akumabari	Protecting from demon

IAIDO TOHO

Toho means the sword methods that were selected from five different Iaido schools.

Each set has a unique character Kiai involved in each form's last cut.

Toho forms and their schools are as follows:

1. Maegiri (Muso Jikiden Eishin-Ryu)	Forward cut
2. Zengogiri (Mugai-Ryu)	Forward and rearward cut
3. Kiriage (Shindo Munen-Ryu)	Reverse cut
4. Shihogiri (Suio-Ryu)	Four directional cut
5. Kissaki Gaeshi (Hoki-Ryu)	Tip flip

UNDERLYING PRINCIPLES

The following quotes illustrate the underlying principles of Iaido and reveal it's true nature. It is my hope that they will inspire you and further your understanding. Bahman Ebrahimi

"I humbly present my thoughts to you on the following matters and pray that you do not think of me as one who would consider himself as wise as you." (page 14)

Your esteemed servant
Hidetomo Nakadai
The Shogun's Scroll
by Stephen F. Kaufman

"There are many things to know, and there are many things to learn. It is a never ending process." (page 18)

The Shogun's Scroll
by Stephen F. Kaufman

"When a man has accomplished his goal it is easy for him to slip into the morass of three deadly attitudes-arrogance, conceit, and false pride.....will show your mettle and not permit self flattery to develop." (page 121)

Hidetomo Nakadai
The Shogun's Scroll
by Stephen F. Kaufman

"How can you make this line shorter?" Master Parker said.
Joe Hyams.....concluded cutting the line in many pieces.
Parker nodded. "It is always better to improve and strengthen your own line or knowledge than to try and cut your opponent's line." (page 36)

Zen in the Martial Arts
by Joe Hyams

Stepping on the Sword

" *The idea of stepping on your opponent's striking sword with your foot is to defeat him the moment he strikes, preventing him from striking a second time. Stepping should not be limited to your feet, but whether doing so with your body, mind, or of course, your sword......It does not mean attacking at the same time......It is taking your action immediately upon your opponent's action." (page 104)*

The Book of Five Rings
Miyamoto Musashi
William Scott Wilson

"There are other styles that.....put virtue in the length of the sword and think they can win.....because of their weak heart.....There are many examples of small forces defeating large ones. In my martial art, we dislike such one-sideness and narrowness." (page 127-128)
"The knowledge of many sword techniques is for the sake of impressing the beginners.....In this world, there are no extraordinary ways of cutting someone down." (page 131-132)
"There is no change in your steps in my martial art. It is like your usual walking on a road." (page 137)

The Book of Five Rings
Miyamoto Musashi
William Scott Wilson

Self Examination and Self Discipline

"A man of mettle should always examine himself and consider where his disposition is underdeveloped, calculate when personal likes and dislikes cause prejudice, and discipline himself to spur himself on where he is underdeveloped." (page 64)

Samurai Wisdom
by Yamaga Soko
Thomas Cleary

"Never lose sight of your own fault." "To be aware of one's faults from moment to moment and to work at this for one's whole life is what is called the "way". Master Konan *(page 67)*

The Art of Samurai
by Yamamoto Tsunetomo
Barry D. Steben

Bushido the Way of the Warrior
"The way of the samurai is found in death. When it comes…..We all want to live…..but not having attained our aim and continuing to live is cowardice…if by setting one's heart right every morning and evening, one is able to live as though his body were already dead, he gains freedom in the way."
(page 53)

Hagakure
Samurai the Code of the Warrior
by Thomas Louis and Thomas Ito

The mysterious skills of the old cat "so what is the technique I use?" Mushin _ I naturally respond in a state 'no_mind.' *(page 21)*

The Samurai Mind
Christopher Hellman

"To be purposeless is not the same as being aimless. Your mind originally has no form, so you should not clutter it with thought…..It is because we are present that there is an opponent. If we are not there, there is no opponent…if your mind has no form, it can have no opposition." *(page 23)*
(The mysterious skills of the old cat.)

The Samurai Mind

"As you know, those who know do not speak; those who speak do not know." *(page 21)*

The Samurai Mind

NO MIND   NO EGO

"Once a person is in a state of Mushin/Muga, accomplishing a task is as easy as thinking it. The state of achieving victory is just to bring out the single mind." *(page 74)*

The Samurai Mind

"The wise man aims to free himself from the boundaries of skill." *(page 27)*

The Samurai Mind

"The potential of drawing the sword and cutting down the opponent is present while the sword is still sheathed. (Saya no Uchi) it is Iaido spirit." *(page 77)*

The Samurai Mind

"Speed ideally comes from within calm." *(page 65)*

The Samurai Mind
by Christopher Hellman

Your mind and your vision should be perfectly free to flow as water does. (page 97)

Samurai Strategies by Michihiro Matsumoto
Boye Lafayette De Mente

"Whether you are walking, standing still, sitting down or reclining, in your conduct and manner you carry yourself in a way that exemplifies a genuine warrior." (page 11)

Code of the Samurai
A Modern Translation of Bushido Shoshinshu of Taira Shige suke
Thomas Cleary
Oscar Ratti

"A white jacket, only needs to be washed once or twice a year, but the human heart, even if cleaned constantly twenty four hours a day, whatever you are doing, in all situations, still becomes dirty again easily.....This is the warrior's ultimate secret of cleaning the heart." (page 78)

Code of the Samurai
A Modern Translation of the Bushido Shoshinshu of Taira Shige suke
Thomas Cleary
Oscar Ratti

"In the way of nurturing life, too much self -confidence is taboo...For example, if you are overconfident in the ability of your blade to cut well, your blade may break when you put it to use. If you are overly confident in the strength of your own chi and put unreasonable demands on it, your chi will lose its force." (page 61)

Yojokun by Kaibara Ekiken
William Scott Willson

"When the mind is inactive, it is empty; when emptiness is active, it is mind. Emptiness goes into action...you should strike emptiness." (page 79)

Soul of the Samurai
Thomas Cleary

Sickness

"To be obsessed even with winning is sickness.
To be obsessed even with using martial arts is sickness.
To be obsessed with showing all one has learned is sickness too.
To be obsessed with offence is sickness; to be obsessed with defence is also sickness.
To become rigidly obsessed with getting rid of sickness is also sickness.
To fix the mind obsessively on anything is considered sickness." (page 46)

Soul of the Samurai
By Thomas Cleary

Where to set the mind?

"If you set your mind on an opponent's physical action, your mind is taken up by the opponent's physical actions. If you set your mind on an opponent's sword, your mind is taken up by the opponent's sword. If you set your mind on the intent to kill an opponent, your mind is taken up by the intent to kill the opponent. If you set your mind on your own sword, your mind is taken up by your sword. If you set your mind on the determination not to get killed, your mind is taken up by the intention not to get killed. If you set your mind on the other's stance, your mind is taken up by the other's stance. The point is that there is nowhere at all to set the mind." (page 117)

Soul of the Samurai
By Thomas Cleary

My wish for you is the peace that comes from a life without ego, an empty mind, and a caring heart.

Bahman Ebrahimi

ABOUT THE AUTHOR

I humbly add my name to those before me who have written about this majestic art. I applaud their work and hope that in some small way I am able to encourage others to pursue the path of the life-giving sword.

Bahman Ebrahimi

Bahman Ebrahimi is the founder and chief instructor of Ken Shin Dojo. He has followed the path of martial arts for most of his life. His dedication has led him to the following accomplishments:
Iaido, 4th Dan
Kickboxing, 4th Dan
Japanese Jujutsu, 3rd Dan
Aikido, Black Belt
Kodokan Judo, Black Belt
Taekwondo, 5th Dan.
He has also completed his B.A. in Interpersonal Communication. He hopes to continue to explore and grow and take you with him on his journey.

Acknowledgments

I would like to express my sincere appreciation to those who volunteered their time and expertise to help make this book a reality.

Billie Wong, photography

Esmaeil Goltapeh, graphic design

Sensei Hiro Inoue, mentor

Robert Harris, editing

Emptiness and the Life - Giving Sword

In Iaido, as in life, the concept of emptiness is very important. An empty mind prepares you for learning. It creates openness to new ideas and new possibilities. It is a mind that can let go of the past and rigid ways of thinking. With this openness, you can discover a sense of freedom, perhaps greater than anything previously experienced. The sword that we examine is not intended to harm or destroy. In fact, it is a life-giving sword. It does not judge. Its purpose is not to create fear. Nor is it intended to cut objects or to take a life. Its purpose is simply to forge the soul and mind of the person who wields it. To know your sword is to know yourself. When both your sword and your mind are free of everything, then you will achieve true emptiness. Then you will understand Emptiness and the Life-Giving Sword.

(B. Ebrahimi & Robert Harris)

May this book serve as your entry to the path of Iaido. I trust that you will preserve and promote this art with a peaceful heart and sincere respect.

When both your sword and your mind are free of everything, then you will achieve true emptiness. Then you will understand Emptiness and the Life-Giving Sword.
Bahman Ebrahimi

EMPTINESS
AND THE LIFE - GIVING SWORD
Bahman Ebrahimi

ISBN 978-1-4992-7134-8

US/CAN: $ 24.99

29042214R00039

Printed in Great Britain
by Amazon